8/05

WI

GEOGRAPHY FACT FILES

OCEANS

John Woodward

A⁺
Smart Apple Media

GEOGRAPHY FACT FILES

First published in 2004 by Hodder Wayland

338 Euston Road, London NW1 3BH, United Kingdom

Hodder Wayland is an imprint of Hodder Children's
Books, a division of Hodder Headline Limited. This
edition published under license from Hodder Children's
Books. All rights reserved.

Produced for Hodder Wayland by

Monkey Puzzle Media Ltd

Gissing's Farm, Fressingfield, Suffolk IP21 5SH

United Kingdom

Copyright © 2004 Hodder Wayland

Editor	Nicola Edwards
Designer	Jamie Asher
Picture Researcher	Sally Cole
Illustrator	Michael Posen
Consultant	Michael Allaby

Published in the United States by Smart Apple Media

2140 Howard Drive West

North Mankato, Minnesota 56003

Library of Congress Cataloging-in-Publication Data

Woodward, John.

Oceans / by John Woodward.

p. cm. — (Geography fact files)

Includes bibliographical references and index.

ISBN 1-58340-427-9

1. Oceanography—Juvenile literature. [1. Oceanography.

2. Ocean.] I. Title. II. Series.

GC21.5.W65 2004

551.46—dc22   2003067393

9 8 7 6 5 4 3 2 1

Acknowledgements

We are grateful to the following for permission to
reproduce photographs: Alamy 11 top
(GreecePhoto.com); AKG-Images 6, 7; Corbis back cover
left (Rick Doyle), 15 bottom (Michael S Yamashita), 23
(Rick Doyle), 25 bottom (Wolfgang Kaehler), 38
(Bohemian Nomad Picturemakers); FLPA 27 (Minden
Pictures); Getty Images 1 (Taxi/Georgette Douwma), 30
(Taxi/Georgette Douwma); Mary Evans Picture Library 8,
9; NASA 21; Nature Picture Library 3 bottom (Jeff
Rotman), 5 top (NASA), 15 top (Albert Aanensen), 31
(Peter Scoones), 34 (Conrad Maufe), 36 (Staffan
Widstrand), 37 (Jeff Rotman), 40 (Peter Scoones), 42
(Michael Pitts); Oxford Scientific Films 3 middle (Harold
Taylor), 5 bottom (Liz Bomford), 17 top Hjalmar
Badarson), 26 both (Harold Taylor), 32 (Duncan Murrell),
33 (Richard Herrmann); PA Photos 43 top (EPA);
Photodisc Collection front cover (Getty Images); Science
Photo Library 3 top (W Haxby/Lamont-Doherty Earth
Observatory), 11 bottom (W Haxby/Lamont-Doherty
Earth Observatory), 16 (Dr Ken Macdonald), 18 (Dr Ken
Macdonald), 19 bottom (Geoff Lane/CSIRO), 22 (Bernard
Edmaier), 35 top (Dr Ken Macdonald); Still Pictures 12
(Klein/Hubert), 25 top (G Griffiths/Christian Aid), 28 (Fred
Bavendam), 29 (Penny Tweedie), 35 bottom (Norbert
Wu), 39 (Jorgen Schytte), 41 (Pierre Gleizes), 43 bottom
(David Drain), 44 (Klaus Andrews), 45 (Andy Crump).

Title page picture: A sea urchin among a forest of giant
seaweed, or kelp.

CONTENTS

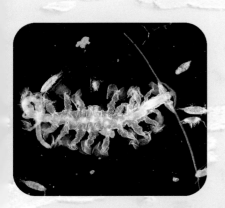

WHAT ARE OCEANS?

Most of Earth is covered by vast, windswept expanses of saltwater called oceans. They are full of life, much of it weird and wonderful. Yet the oceans are also desolate, dangerous places that humans have barely begun to explore.

MASSIVE AND MYSTERIOUS

The oceans are huge. They cover 70 percent of Earth's surface, and in places they are deep enough to swallow Mount Everest with nearly a mile to spare. They hold immense volumes of water, the substance that is essential to the survival of all living things. Life on Earth probably began in the oceans, and salty ocean water is rich in the chemicals that make up the bodies of living things. But because humans breathe air, the oceans are difficult to explore. As a result, people know less about the deep oceans than they know about the surface of the moon.

FACT FILE

OCEAN STATISTICS
• The oceans and shallow coastal seas cover an area of 141 million square miles (361 million sq km).
• The deep oceans cover about 117 million square miles (300 million sq km).
• The average depth of the oceans is 12,234 feet (3,730 m).

The oceans have been created as **continents** have moved apart and drifted around the globe.

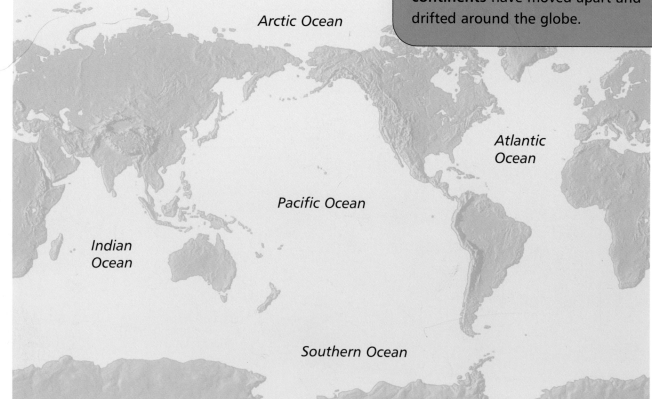

Arctic Ocean

Atlantic Ocean

Pacific Ocean

Indian Ocean

Southern Ocean

A view of Earth from above southern Africa shows the vast size of the blue oceans compared to the land.

WHAT MAKES AN OCEAN?

Many small seas are just parts of continents that have become flooded. If their water drained away, they would soon look just like the surrounding landscape. But an ocean is not just a vast expanse of saltwater. It is a low-lying section of Earth's **crust** that is made of a special type of rock, quite different from the rock that forms continents. So even if it had no water in it at all, an ocean would be special.

About 200 million years ago, all the continents were joined together in one great land mass. This was surrounded by a single huge ocean that covered the rest of the planet. Since then the continents have moved apart. New oceans have been created between them, including the Atlantic, Indian, and Arctic Oceans, and the icy Southern Ocean that surrounds Antarctica. The original huge ocean has shrunk as a result, but it is still the biggest ocean on Earth: the mighty Pacific.

The tropical ocean waters of the Great Barrier Reef in Australia are swarming with life. Yet for humans, an ocean is an alien environment, like the atmosphere of another planet.

OCEAN EXPLORATION

The early ocean explorers had no way of investigating below the ocean surface. But they traveled across the globe on amazing voyages in their fragile sailing ships. Gradually, they mapped the oceans of the world. The more they traveled, the more they learned about how oceans work.

AT THE START

The first ocean explorers left no record of their travels. They included people such as the Polynesians of the Pacific, who began exploring and settling the Pacific islands more than 3,500 years ago. They must have discovered a lot about the ocean **currents** and winds, simply to find their way.

On the other side of the world, the Scandinavian Vikings began exploring the cold waters of the North Atlantic in about A.D. 850. They soon discovered Iceland and Greenland. In about 985, they even sailed to North America, 500 years before Columbus.

PIONEERS AND SCIENTISTS

Columbus set sail from Spain across the Atlantic in 1492. By then, people realized that the world was round, and Columbus was hoping to discover a short route to the rich Spice Islands of the East Indies. But America was in the way, so instead he arrived among the islands of the Caribbean, which are still called the West Indies.

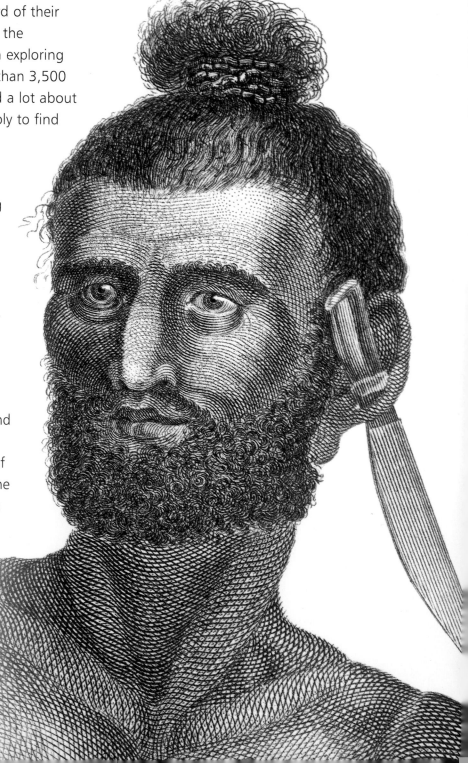

Ocean explorers such as Captain James Cook discovered unknown peoples as well as lands during their voyages.

The Atlantic voyage of Columbus was followed by the first voyage around the world. Ferdinand Magellan left Spain in 1519, aiming to reach the Spice Islands by sailing around South America and across the Pacific. He meant to come back the same way, but when he was killed in the Philippines, his crew decided to keep going. They crossed the Indian Ocean, sailed around Africa, and back into the Atlantic.

FILLING THE GAPS

By the 18th century, the oceans were quite well mapped, but there were still big gaps in the south. Scientific explorers such as Louis de Bougainville and James Cook set out to fill the gaps by making long zigzag voyages in search of new lands. By 1800, the picture was virtually complete, and only the icebound coasts of Antarctica were still uncharted.

FACT FILE

THE DEADLY OCEAN

• Magellan left Spain in September 1519 with 265 men. Exactly four years later, just 18 returned.

• The man who brought Magellan's ship back to Spain, Juan Sebastian d'Elcano, led a second voyage in 1524. He started with 450 men, but just 9 survived.

• From 1577 to 1580, Francis Drake sailed around the world. He started out with 164 men and came back with 59.

Dating from about 1519, this Portuguese chart of the northern Atlantic is surprisingly accurate.

7

INTO THE DEEP

The first people to explore the ocean depths worked entirely from the surface, using instruments lowered from ships. Much of today's knowledge still comes from equipment on ships and even satellites. But the invention of deep-diving gear has given scientists a chance to see the submarine world for themselves.

EXPLORING THE OCEANS

In 1872, the first real effort was made to explore the oceans themselves, and not just cross them. The British research ship *HMS Challenger* sailed the oceans for more than three years, traveling 69,000 nautical miles (79,360 miles [128,000 km]). The scientists on board measured ocean depths and temperatures, and took samples of the water and the ocean floors. They collected 4,000 new types of marine life from every depth, even as far as 26,240 feet (8,000 m) below the surface.

The expedition marked the birth of a new science called oceanography. Since then, many other ships have continued the work, using similar methods. But they also use electronic technology such as side-scan **echo-sounders** to measure depths precisely, and the information has allowed oceanographers to make detailed maps of the ocean floors. **Orbiting** satellites have been used for the same job, and to make images of the clouds of **plankton** that drift near the ocean surface.

LOCATION FILE

THE CHALLENGER DEEP
The deepest spot in any ocean is the Challenger Deep, in the eastern Pacific. It is named after the British survey ship Challenger II, which located it off the Mariana Islands in 1951. A super-accurate echo-sounder used by a Japanese survey ship in 1984 measured its maximum depth as 35,827 feet (10,923 m).

Scientists examine a haul of specimens brought up from the deep sea during the *Challenger* expedition of 1872–75.

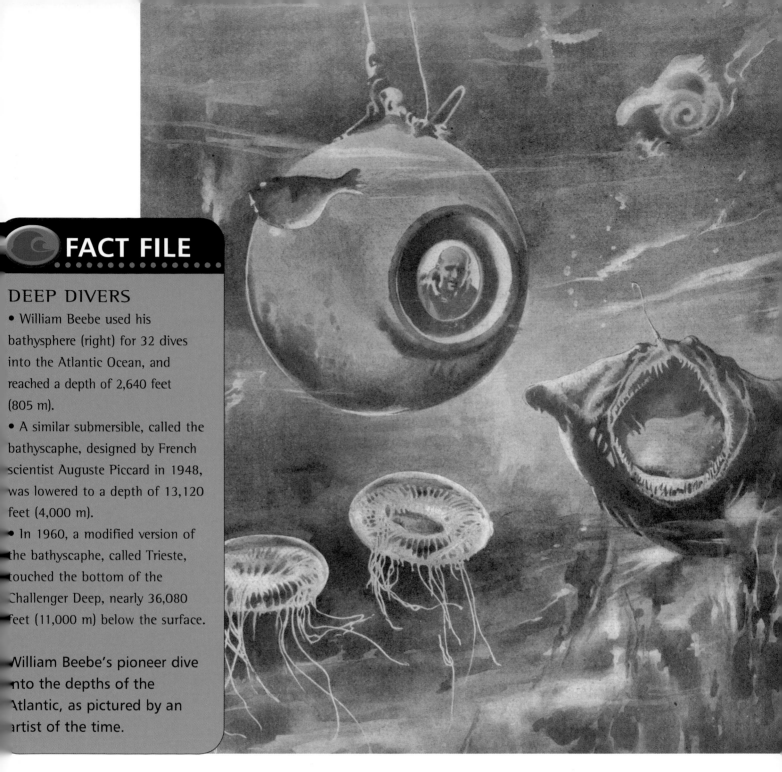

DIVING INTO THE DARK

People have been using diving equipment to explore shallow water for at least 200 years. But the deep oceans were beyond reach until 1930, when the American scientist Dr. William Beebe was lowered into the Atlantic in a steel ball equipped with very thick glass windows, called the bathysphere. It was the first deep-sea **submersible**, designed to protect its crew from the crushing pressure of deep water.

Similar submersibles have since reached the very deepest parts of the oceans, suspended on long cables from the surface. But the most useful craft are able to move under their own power to investigate underwater features. They are fitted with powerful lights, cameras, mechanical grabs, and other sampling equipment so they can bring back pictures and samples from the deep ocean. They give their crews a first-hand view of the deep-sea world.

SUBMARINE WORLD

At the edges of the continents the sea is quite shallow, but within a few miles of land it starts to slope downward into the black depths. At the bottom is the ocean floor, a fantastic submarine world of great plains, deep chasms, huge mountains, and even active volcanoes.

THE CONTINENTAL SHELF

The continents are like great slabs of rock, laid on Earth's crust like giant paving stones. The oceans lie all around them, and powerful waves have worn away their edges to make cliffs, bays, and beaches. This "erosion" cuts back the continental rock at wave level, but leaves a lot of it intact underwater. The result is a shallow sea at the edge of the ocean, covering a ledge of rock called the **continental shelf**.

The continental shelf slopes gently down toward the original edge of the continent. In some places, such as eastern Africa, this may not be far from the coast. In others, like western Europe, it may extend for many miles. But at the edge, the seabed falls away more steeply. This is called the continental slope. In some places, such as off the east coast of the U.S., the continental slope contains huge canyons 2,952 feet (900 m) deep.

FACT FILE

SHELVES, SLOPES, AND TRENCHES

- The sea over a continental shelf has an average depth of 426 feet (130 m).
- The edge of a continental shelf is about 984 feet (300 m) below the waves.
- The continental slope descends from about 984 to 9,840 feet (300–3,000 m) below sea level.
- The continental rise slopes gently from 9,840 to 13,120 feet (3,000–4,000 m) below sea level.
- The deepest **ocean trenches** plunge to nearly 36,080 feet (11,000 m) below sea level.

A section of ocean showing the continental shelf, the ocean floor, a **mid-ocean ridge** and a volcanic island.

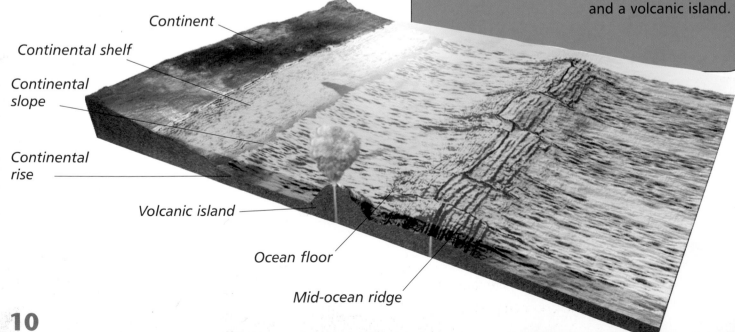

Continent

Continental shelf

Continental slope

Continental rise

Volcanic island

Ocean floor

Mid-ocean ridge

Colossal volcanoes have grown up from the sea floor to create volcanic islands. Some are still active, but others, such as Santorini, in the Mediterranean, have been dormant for centuries.

THE OCEAN FLOOR

At the bottom of the continental slope, the ocean floor is covered with rock debris swept down from above. The debris forms a gentle slope called the continental rise, which leads down to the ocean floor.

Much of the ocean floor is a flat plain, covered with a deep layer of fine ooze. But in places, volcanoes have burst up through the ooze and created huge underwater mountains called seamounts. Some of these reach the ocean surface as volcanic islands, such as Hawaii. Near the middle of most oceans there are long rows of volcanoes that form mid-ocean ridges, and near the edges there are often deep chasms called ocean trenches.

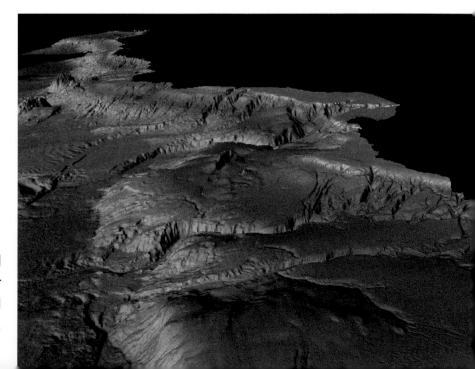

An image of the continental shelf (brown) and ocean floor (blue) off California, created from echo-sounding data.

THE CRUST OF EARTH

Earth's outer crust is like a giant football, made of many separate sections that join together to form a huge rocky sphere. But these sections are not rigidly locked together. They move, causing earthquakes and volcanoes. Over millions of years, these movements have created the world's continents and oceans.

EARTH'S LAYERS

Most of Earth is made up of a thick layer of very heavy, hot rock known as the **mantle**, which surrounds Earth's core. Outside the mantle is a cold, rocky shell called the crust.

Most of the crust is made of a dark, heavy rock called **basalt**. It is much like the mantle rock below, but lighter. Because of this, it "floats" on the mantle, like oil floating on water. It forms the bedrock of the oceans, or the oceanic crust. Some parts of the crust are made of even lighter rock, which forms the continents. This continental crust also "floats" on the mantle. But since it is lighter, it floats at a higher level than the oceanic crust, like an empty boat compared to a boat loaded down with bricks. This is why the continents are higher than the ocean floors.

Basalt occurs on land in Iceland, which has been created by oceanic volcanoes. The dark rock often cracks into strange column shapes as it cools down.

INTO THE EARTH

- Oceanic crust is four to seven miles (6–11 km) thick.
- Continental crust is 16 to 56 miles (25–90 km) thick. The thickest parts lie under great mountain ranges such as the Himalayas.
- The mantle is 1,798 miles (2,900 km) thick, and its temperature ranges from 1,832 to 7,232 °F (1,000 to 4,000 °C).
- Earth's core has two parts. The liquid outer core is 1,395 miles (2,250 km) thick, and the inner core is a ball of solid metal 1,507 miles (2,430 km) across.

![logo] **LOCATION FILE**

THE ALEUTIAN ISLANDS

One of the biggest plates of Earth's crust lies beneath the Pacific Ocean. At its northern edge, the Pacific Plate is sliding under Alaska, and the plate boundary is clearly marked by a chain of volcanoes that loops across the North Pacific. They are called the Aleutian Islands.

MOVING PLATES

Earth's core works like a giant nuclear reactor, producing huge amounts of heat. This heats up the rock of the mantle like soup in a saucepan. When soup is being warmed up, it moves. The hot mantle rock moves in the same way, but very slowly. As it moves, it drags the crust with it. Since the crust is cold and brittle, it breaks into separate, mobile sections called plates.

PUSH AND PULL

In some places, the plates are being pushed together. When one plate slides beneath another, earthquakes and volcanoes occur. Eventually, these volcanoes can form islands and mountain ranges. In other places, the plates are being pulled apart, making great rifts in Earth's crust that, over millions of years, become new oceans.

This map shows how the crust has broken into separate, moving plates.

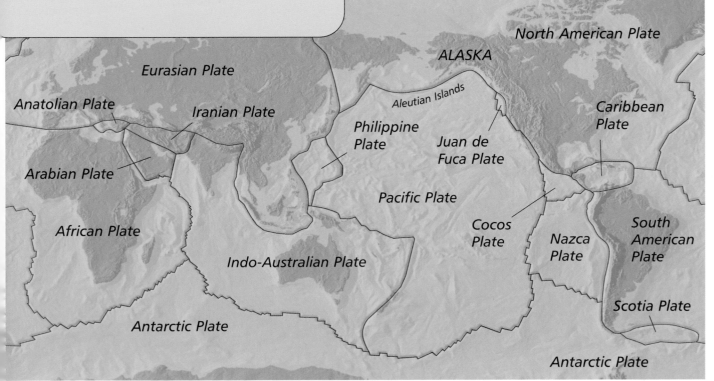

13

FIERY DESTRUCTION

In places where the great plates of Earth's crust are colliding, one plate is usually dragged beneath another. This creates the vast trenches that are the deepest parts of the oceans, and causes earthquakes and volcanic eruptions. But it has also produced the rock that builds continents.

PUSHING AND PULLING

When the crust of Earth moves, the separate plates are pushed together or pulled apart. In places where they are pushed together, the edge of one plate is destroyed as it dives beneath the other plate, down into the hot mantle. The heavier rock that forms an ocean floor always slides beneath the lighter rock of a continent, so the continent stays intact while the edge of the ocean floor is destroyed.

TRENCHES AND VOLCANOES

These destructive boundaries are marked by deep ocean trenches where one plate is being dragged beneath another. But as the plate sinks down into the hot mantle, its rocks melt. The molten rock bursts up through weak points in the edge of the plate above, erupting as volcanoes.

Where ocean crust is diving beneath a continent, the volcanoes help create mountain ranges, such as the Andes of South America. In places where two oceanic plates are colliding, volcanoes erupt to form chains of islands, such as the Aleutians. These chains are called island arcs. Over many millions of years, the islands may become big enough to join up. The continents that people live on today probably originated in this way.

A section through an oceanic plate boundary, showing one ocean plate diving beneath another.

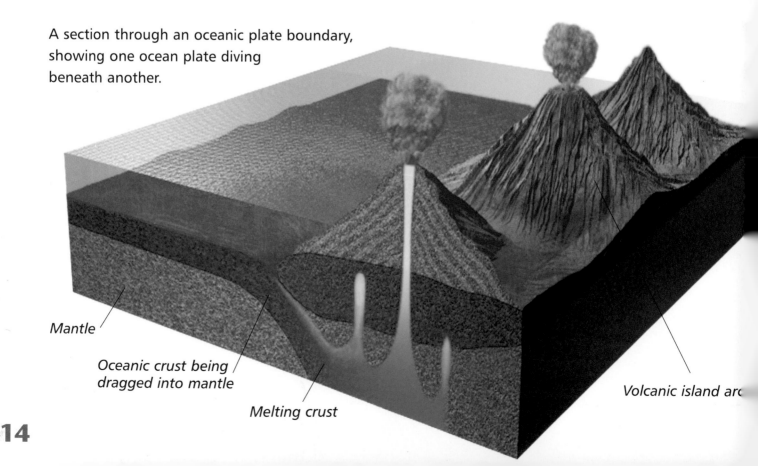

Mantle

Oceanic crust being dragged into mantle

Melting crust

Volcanic island arc

THE PACIFIC RING OF FIRE

Most of the destructive plate boundaries lie around the Pacific Ocean, which is gradually shrinking as its ocean floor is destroyed at the edges. The volcanoes that erupt from the boundaries form an enormous "ring of fire" surrounding the ocean. It extends up the west coast of South and North America, and through the Aleutian Islands to Japan, Southeast Asia, and New Zealand.

This volcano erupting in New Zealand in 1996 is part of the Pacific Ring of Fire.

FACT FILE

PACIFIC EARTHQUAKES

Most of the world's most destructive earthquakes have hit regions around the edge of the Pacific Plate. Their violence is measured on the Richter Scale, and anything measuring 7 or more is catastrophic.

• San Francisco, California	1906	8.2
• Tokyo, Japan	1923	8.2
• Anchorage, Alaska	1964	8.6
• Haicheng, China	1975	7.4
• Tangshan, China	1976	7.6
• Loma Prieta, California	1989	7.0

LOCATION FILE

JAPAN

Perched on the edge of a deep ocean trench in the northwest Pacific, Japan is rocked by more earthquakes than anywhere else on Earth. Tokyo has suffered a serious earthquake every 70 years or so since records began in about 1600. Since the city was last hit by a big earthquake in 1923, another is well overdue.

This factory in Kobe, Japan, was destroyed by an earthquake that hit the city in 1995. The earthquake that is predicted to strike Tokyo is likely to be far more catastrophic.

FILLING THE GAPS

While oceanic crust is being destroyed in some parts of the world, new oceanic crust is being created in others. Liquid basalt is bubbling up from the mantle beneath the deep, dark, cold water and freezing solid to build submarine mountains and fiery islands.

MID-OCEAN RIDGES

As the creeping hot rocks of the mantle drag Earth's plates across the globe, some plates collide, while others are pulled apart. Most of the pulling apart happens in the oceans, along zones called mid-ocean ridges.

These ridges start as ragged tears in the crust. The plates are ripped apart by the forces in the mantle, creating a feature called a **rift valley**. The hard rock collapses into the gap, but meanwhile hot, molten rock wells up from the mantle below.

FACT FILE

THE MID-ATLANTIC RIDGE
• The longest mid-ocean ridge is in the center of the Atlantic Ocean. It is about 6,200 miles (10,000 km) long, and runs all the way from the Arctic to near the Antarctic.
• The submarine mountains of the Mid-Atlantic Ridge are up to 13,120 feet (4,000 m) high. That's half the height of the tallest mountains in the Himalayas.

Deep-sea crabs feed alongside a crack in the ocean floor at a mid-ocean ridge.

ICELAND

Iceland is a part of the Mid-Atlantic Ridge that has appeared above the ocean surface. It is almost entirely made of oceanic basalt that has poured from hundreds of volcanoes. About 20 of these volcanoes are active, and in 1963, a new one erupted from under the sea to create the island of Surtsey.

A fountain of molten basalt explodes from a rift on Krafla, one of the biggest volcanoes on Iceland.

PILLOW LAVA

Mantle rock is normally kept solid by the terrific pressure beneath the crust. But when the crust splits, the pressure is released, and some of the mantle rock melts. It squirts up through the cracks as liquid basalt lava. When it bursts out into the freezing ocean water, the outside of the lava flow turns to solid rock, but the inside is still liquid. It keeps billowing out through cracks in the hard rocky skin of the flow, like toothpaste from a tube, and freezes into cushion-shaped "pillow lavas."

Over millions of years these lava flows have built up chains of submarine mountains. They follow the rifts in the crust for thousands of miles, with a line of mountains on each side of the rift valley. In some places, such as the Galápagos Islands and Iceland, the mountains have reached the surface of the oceans to form strange volcanic landscapes of black basalt.

A section through a mid-ocean ridge, showing the rift valley, ridge mountains, and a volcanic island.

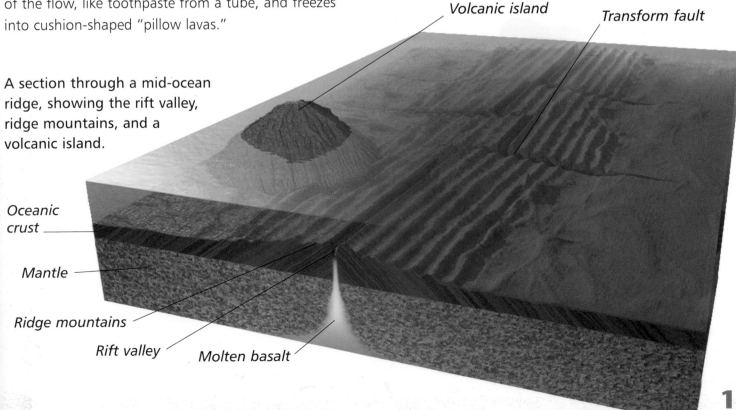

Volcanic island

Transform fault

Oceanic crust

Mantle

Ridge mountains

Rift valley

Molten basalt

MAGNETIC STRIPS

Scientists using sensitive equipment towed behind ships have discovered something strange about the ocean floors. The magnetism of the rock shows that it has been built up in a series of strips, like giant planks, and all the strips line up with the mid-ocean ridges.

NORTH THEN SOUTH

The needle on a compass always points north. But a million years ago, the needle would have pointed south. The magnetism of Earth was reversed. The same thing has happened many times in Earth's history.

When molten rock cools and becomes solid, it records the magnetism of Earth at the time. So the new rock forming at mid-ocean ridges today records "normal" magnetism. But farther away from the ridge on each side, rock that formed a million years ago has reversed magnetism. Farther out still, it is normal again.

This false-color image shows an actual pattern of magnetic reversals near a mid-ocean ridge. The green and blue stripes have reversed magnetism, while the red and yellow stripes are normal.

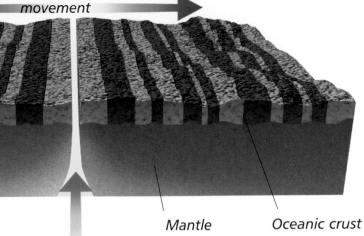

Normal magnetism (brown)

Reversed magnetism (blue)

Plate movement

Mantle

Oceanic crust

Molten basalt

Strips of rock with different magnetism are created at a mid-ocean ridge and move apart at the same rate, so the pattern of strips is the same on each side.

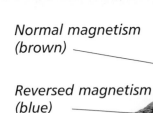

LOCATION FILE

THE JUAN DE FUCA RIDGE

The first proper survey of ocean floor magnetism was made near Vancouver Island, off western North America. A ship towed a magnetometer across the area of the Juan de Fuca mid-ocean ridge. It traveled on a series of east-west tracks five miles (8 km) apart. The magnetic signals were used to map the rocks of the ocean floor.

A MAGNETIC BAR CODE

This strange effect was discovered in the 1950s, by scientists who towed instruments called **magnetometers** behind ships to map the magnetism of the Pacific floor. They found that the rocks with normal and reversed magnetism formed strips, like a bar code. The strips were parallel with a mid-ocean ridge, and the "bar code" on the western side of the ridge was like a reflection of the pattern on the eastern side.

OCEAN FLOORBOARDS

In 1963, a young scientist named Fred Vine suggested that the magnetic strips record the growth of the ocean floor. The normal strips near the ridge are new rock, and the reversed strips farther out are older. The normal strips even farther out are older still. They show that the ocean floor is built up from strips of rock like floorboards, with the newest ones in the middle and the oldest ones at the edges.

FACT FILE

MAGNETIC REVERSAL

• The Earth has had "normal" magnetism for 690,000 years.

• Before this, it had reversed magnetism for about the same period, with a short phase of normal magnetism around 900,000 years ago.

• Similar periods of normal and reversed magnetism are now known for over 80 million years of Earth's history.

• Scientists still do not know why the magnetism of Earth changes.

The magnetism of oceanic crust samples has to be analyzed in a laboratory.

EXPANDING OCEANS

When scientists discovered that ocean floors are built up from rocky strips of different ages, they were able to figure out their history. The results prove that the ocean floors are spreading. They also show that the theory of continental drift, which scientists once laughed at, is true.

CONTINENTAL DRIFT

In 1912, a German scientist named Alfred Wegener came up with an amazing theory. He suggested that the continents of North and South America, Asia, and Africa had once been joined together, and that they had split apart and drifted around the globe. It was called the theory of continental drift.

Most other scientists thought Wegener was wrong, even though his ideas were based on good scientific evidence. But the discovery that the ocean floors are built up from strips of different ages has proved that Wegener was right.

PEOPLE FILE

ALFRED WEGENER
Wegener was not an expert in rocks and earth movements. He was a meteorologist—a weather expert—and a polar explorer. So although his theory was well researched, other scientists didn't take it seriously. He died from a heart attack while crossing the Greenland ice sheet in 1930, so he never lived to see his theory proved.

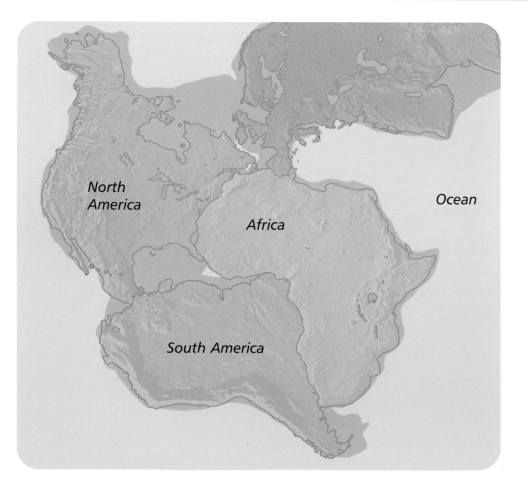

North America

Africa

Ocean

South America

Around 130 million years ago, North America, South America, and Africa were all joined together, and the Atlantic did not exist. The dark blue areas are continental shelves, which were probably dry land.

THE RED SEA

Strangely, mid-ocean ridges can develop under continents. One plate splits into two, and as the two parts are pulled apart, a new ocean begins to form. This is happening in the Great Rift Valley of East Africa. The northern end of the Valley has already opened up to become the Red Sea.

Above: **This satellite view of the northern Red Sea shows how Arabia (on the left) has torn away from Africa to create a huge, forked rift valley. The valley will eventually form a new ocean.**

If the ocean floor is not being consumed at the edges, it will get bigger and bigger. This is happening in the South Atlantic, which is spreading from the Mid-Atlantic Ridge and growing about .8 inches (2 cm) wider every year. That may not seem much, but over 110 million years it has been enough to split South America from Africa and create an ocean.

THE SPREADING ATLANTIC

Strips of ocean floor are created at a mid-ocean ridge, from new basalt erupting from below. As the forces in the mantle pull the ridge apart, the strips move away on each side, and more molten rock wells up to make new strips. Gradually the strips move farther away from the ridge.

THE SHRINKING PACIFIC

The spreading rate is twice as fast in parts of the Pacific Ocean. But as new ocean floor is created, old ocean floor is dragged down into the deep ocean trenches around the Pacific Rim and destroyed. The old rocks are being destroyed faster than the new rocks are created, so the Pacific is shrinking.

OCEAN WATER

The vast quantities of water in the oceans were created early in the history of the planet, when it was still a lifeless ball of hot rock. Originally full of foul-smelling chemicals, the water gradually became the rich, salty liquid that enabled life to develop on Earth.

THE FIRST OCEAN

Soon after the Earth was formed 4,600 million years ago, huge clouds of hot gases poured out from inside the planet and erupted from volcanoes. The gases probably included vast amounts of water vapor that formed great clouds around Earth, much like the clouds that surround Venus today. But as Earth's surface cooled, the water vapor turned into rain that poured down to create the first ocean.

The water in the early ocean probably smelled strongly of chlorine, like a swimming pool. Chlorine is one of the gases produced by volcanoes, and it dissolves easily in water. But over time, rainwater flowing off the early continents added more substances to the oceans, including a metal called sodium, which mixes with chlorine to make sodium chloride, or salt. This is why ocean water is salty.

Steam erupting from the top of a volcano on Kamchatka, in Siberia. The water that fills oceans may have come from volcanoes.

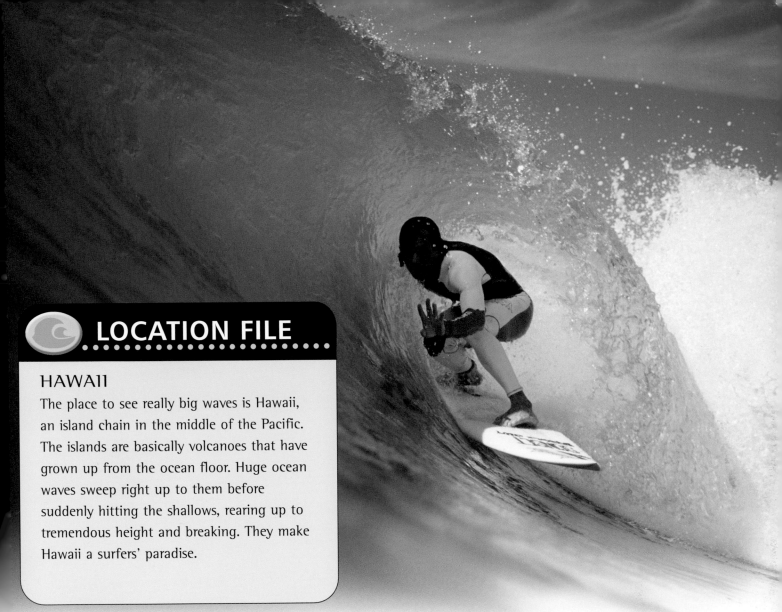

OCEAN WAVES

Apart from its saltiness, the most obvious thing about ocean water is its violence. Great waves roll across the ocean surface, to break upon the shore with shattering force. They are formed by the wind blowing across the ocean. They start as ripples that travel across the surface, growing bigger all the time.

Although waves move forward, the water in them does not. It just goes up and down as the wave passes. A seabird, for example, floating on the sea, rises up and over each wave, without moving forward at all. If the water were moving, the bird would move with it. The water itself moves forward only when the wave breaks, and its crest plunges onto the shore.

A surfer rides an ocean wave as it reaches the end of its journey and breaks on a shallow shore.

TIDES AND CURRENTS

Ocean water is always on the move. It is pulled this way and that by the gravity of the moon, and swirls around the globe in powerful currents. The movement carries warm water toward the poles and cold water to the tropics, and moderates the extremes of temperature, making the planet a more comfortable place to live.

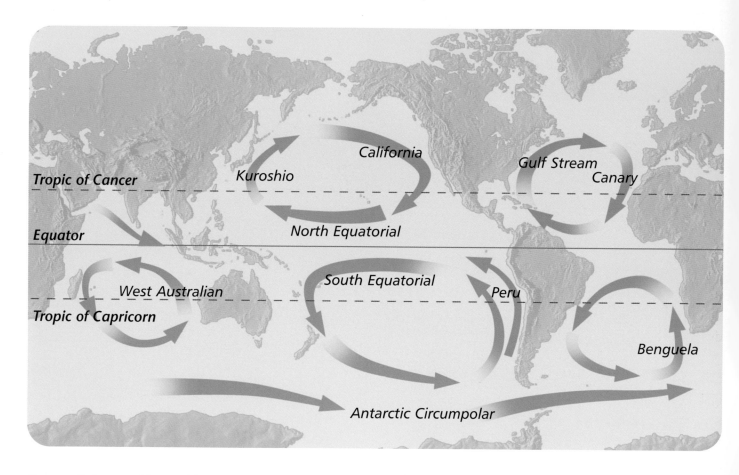

Tropic of Cancer

Equator

Tropic of Capricorn

Kuroshio *California*

North Equatorial

Gulf Stream *Canary*

West Australian

South Equatorial *Peru*

Benguela

Antarctic Circumpolar

Some of the world's major ocean currents, showing how cold water moves toward the equator, and warm water toward the poles.

THE MOON AND TIDES

As the moon orbits Earth, it pulls ocean water toward it. A "hump" of ocean water follows the moon around, balanced by another "hump" on the other side of the world. This causes two high **tides** a day, with two low tides in between. As the water rises and falls, it also flows in and out of channels and along coasts.

SWIRLING CURRENTS

Tides are obvious only near coasts, but currents affect the whole ocean. Many currents are driven by winds, and by the rotation of Earth. The combination creates huge swirling eddies in the oceans. In the north, these circular currents move clockwise. They flow westward along the equator, alongside similar currents that swirl counter-clockwise to the south.

One of the most powerful southern currents is the Peru Current, which flows north up the western coast of South America. It carries cold water all

Floods in Kenya in 1998 were probably caused by changed weather patterns brought about by an El Niño event in the Pacific Ocean.

the way to the equator. There it turns west, and meets warm water flowing from the west. But sometimes the winds driving the cold current slow down, allowing the warm water to push farther southeast than usual. This is called **El Niño**, and if it lasts a long time, it can cause all kinds of problems by destroying the food supplies of ocean wildlife, and disrupting the climate and causing droughts or floods on land.

DEEP FLOW

Other ocean currents flow across the ocean floors. For example, in the Arctic, ocean water freezes at the surface, chilling the water below. The water beneath the ice also gets saltier, because when seawater freezes, its salt is driven out. Since this cold, very salty water is heavier than the rest of the ocean water, a current of cold water sinks and flows south along the floor of the North Atlantic. The surface water is replaced by warmer water drawn north from near the Gulf of Mexico, in a current called the **Gulf Stream**.

 LOCATION FILE

WINTER WARMER

Northern Europe is as far north as Labrador, in Canada, and Mongolia, in Central Asia. But it is far warmer than either. One reason is the Gulf Stream, the ocean current that draws warm water north from near Florida. The warm water heats up the air above the ocean and gives Europe comfortable temperatures in the winter.

The formation of sea ice in the northeastern Atlantic makes surface water sink, drawing warm surface water north to take its place.

RICHES FROM THE DEEP

Ocean currents do a lot more than move water from one part of the world to another. They also carry the substances that feed the tiny plant-like algae that live near the ocean surface. Since these algae are an essential part of the web of life in the oceans, the currents keep the oceans alive.

PLANKTON

Many of the **minerals** that lie on the ocean floor are vital to microscopic algae that drift in the ocean. They form part of a floating community of algae and animals called plankton. The algae are known as **phytoplankton**. They are eaten by drifting animals called **zooplankton**, which themselves feed small fish and other animals. The small fish are eaten by bigger fish, so eventually most of the animals in the ocean depend on phytoplankton.

Most phytoplankton are beautiful glass-like single-celled algae that can be seen only through a microscope.

Zooplankton include tiny shrimp-like copepods and the young forms of animals such as crabs, barnacles, and mussels.

MINERAL DELIVERY

Phytoplankton need light to survive. They must live in the sunlit surface layers of the ocean, so they cannot get at the minerals lying on the ocean floor. But luckily they have a delivery service. When cold water sinks and flows along the bottom of the ocean, it scoops up mineral particles. In places called upwelling zones, this cold water comes to the surface, and it brings the minerals with it.

Many upwelling zones are near continents swept by powerful coastal currents. The currents draw surface water away from the shore, and it is replaced by mineral-rich water welling up from below. Something similar happens at the equator, where surface water is drawn away by equatorial currents. Near the poles, winter storms do the same job. As a result, the oceans in these places are rich in minerals and teeming with marine life.

OCEAN DESERTS

By contrast, other ocean regions are virtually dead. Where there is no upwelling, the water contains hardly any minerals. There is little plankton and very few fish. So while the water may be a beautiful clear blue, it is little more than an ocean desert.

LOCATION FILE

THE GALÁPAGOS
The Galápagos Islands lie on the equator, off South America. They lie in an upwelling zone that makes them rich in marine life such as seabirds. But in some years, a severe El Niño event (see page 25) stops the upwelling water from reaching the surface. The food supply runs out, and many seabirds may starve to death.

Above: The blue-footed boobies that nest on the volcanic slopes of the Galápagos rely on plankton-rich ocean currents to keep them supplied with fish.

27

OCEAN GARDENS

Most ocean wildlife depends on the tiny algae that drift near the surface as phytoplankton. If there are no phytoplankton, animals have nothing to eat. But in warm, shallow seas, animals and algae work together in a different way to create dazzling underwater gardens of life called coral reefs.

SUGAR FROM SUNLIGHT

The microscopic algae that live in the plankton have a clever trick. They use the energy of sunlight to turn water and dissolved air into sugar. All green plants can do the same thing. They make food out of virtually nothing. And by eating the algae, animals get the food they need, too. This is why the plankton are so vital to ocean life.

This coral reef in New Guinea supports a huge variety of life, like an underwater rainforest.

PERFECT PARTNERS

Plankton are scarce in many tropical seas. But animals called corals are able to grow algae under their transparent skins. The algae have somewhere safe to live, and they supply the corals with sugar. The corals are also able to catch small animals and eat them. They pass some of this food to the algae, to make up for the lack of minerals in the water. They are perfect partners.

CORAL REEFS

Corals are much like the sea anemones that attach themselves to rocks on the seashore. But they grow like plants, forming great masses of corals that are all attached to each other. They are often supported by rocky skeletons made of chalky limestone. Over the centuries, the skeletons build up into great rocky reefs, covered with live corals.

In the South Pacific, many coral reefs grow around volcanic islands. Some of these volcanoes have gradually sunk beneath the waves, but the corals have continued to grow to create low, circular reefs around quiet lagoons, called atolls. Fish and other animals graze on the algae growing on the reefs. Other fish hunt the smaller animals. The corals feed on the remains of their meals. Reefs are like underwater wildlife parks in the middle of the ocean.

 LOCATION FILE

THE GREAT BARRIER REEF

The largest coral reef system in the world is the Great Barrier Reef (above), which extends along the northeast coast of Australia. It is made up of more than 2,500 separate reefs and is more than 1,240 miles (2,000 km) long. It is the biggest structure ever built by living things, and it can even be seen from space!

Above: **The vast size of the Great Barrier Reef can be appreciated only from the air. Here reef flats of living coral enclose shallow lagoons of clear, blue water and coral sand.**

FACT FILE

REEF FACTS

• Some coral reefs have been growing for 50 million years and are more than 3,280 feet (1,000 m) thick.
• There may be up to two million microscopic algae living in each .2 square inches (1 sq cm) of coral.
• The biggest coral atoll is Kwajalein, in the western Pacific. It is 43 miles (70 km) long and 19 miles (30 km) wide.

THE SHALLOW SEAS

For most ocean wildlife, the best places to live are the shallow seas near the continents. This is partly because the water contains a lot of the minerals needed by plankton. Light can also reach right down to the seabed, allowing seaweeds to grow. They create underwater forests, full of food and life.

A RICH SOUP

The continental shelves are covered by shallow seas less than 984 feet (300 m) deep. Compared with the deep, dark oceans, these seas are teeming with life. Many upwelling currents (see page 27) come to the surface near coasts. They supply minerals that feed the tiny algae in the plankton. More minerals flow off the land in rivers. So the algae grow well, and so do the creatures that eat them.

A sea urchin grazes on the root-like holdfasts of giant seaweeds growing in the sunlit shallows, scraping away small algae and animals.

THE LIVING SEABED

Many of these animals live on the seabed, often among thick forests of seaweed. All seaweeds are algae, like phytoplankton, but they grow much bigger. The giant seaweeds that grow in the eastern Pacific can grow 328 feet (100 m) high! Like phytoplankton, they need light to make food, so they grow only in shallow, sunlit seas.

Many shallow-sea animals spend their lives rooted to one spot like seaweeds. They include all kinds of clams, worms, and anemones that sieve the rich water for tiny food particles, or catch small creatures in their stinging tentacles.

FACT FILE

SHALLOW SEA LIFE
• Thirty-five cubic feet (1 cu m) of water in a rich shallow sea can contain more than 400 million tiny planktonic plants and animals.
• Only about two percent of known marine animal species live in the deep oceans. Most of the other 98 percent live in shallow seas.
• Most of the fish and shellfish caught by the world's fishing fleets are caught in shallow seas.

Anemones use their stinging tentacles to gather food particles from the plankton-rich water of shallow seas.

UNDERWATER HUNTERS

The worms and clams that live on the seabed are eaten by crabs and lobsters that walk around among the rocks and seaweeds, and by flatfish and rays that swim over the sand. Bigger fish, such as cod and grouper, snap up the smaller ones, and these are attacked by hungry sharks and sea lions. Meanwhile, great shoals of mid-water fish, such as herring, mackerel, and anchovy, feast on the plankton in the water above—and are caught by humans for food.

 LOCATION FILE

THE GRAND BANKS

One of the richest continental shelf seas lies off Newfoundland, in eastern Canada. It is a huge area called the Grand Banks. The seabed is only about 492 feet (150 m) below the surface, and is swept by the warm Gulf Stream current. It supports masses of marine life, and is one of the world's most important fishing grounds.

THE OPEN OCEANS

Compared with the shelf seas, the open oceans can seem almost lifeless. But in places where the water is rich in minerals, the surface water can be thick with phytoplankton. This provides food for the millions of tiny animals that form the zooplankton, which act as bait for all sorts of ocean hunters.

VITAL MINERALS

The deep ocean water beyond the continental shelves contains far less life than the shallow seas. There is much less plankton in the water, and some tropical areas may have almost none at all. This means there is nothing for larger animals to eat, so they cannot survive. But in cooler oceans, winter storms bring vital minerals to the surface. They trigger huge "blooms" of algae in spring and summer. The algae are eaten by swarms of microscopic animals that drift near the surface, and these swarms attract plankton-eating fish.

SILVER SHOALS

Many of the plankton-eaters are small fish such as herring, anchovy, and mackerel, which swim in great shoals. As they swim through the plankton, they open their mouths so the water flows through their gills. Gills are the feathery, blood-filled structures at the back of a fish's head that gather oxygen from the water. The delicate gills are protected by fine net-like filters called gill rakers, which catch the plankton like tea-strainers. Huge plankton-eating fish such as the basking shark and manta ray use the same system.

FACT FILE

OCEAN HUNTERS

• The fastest hunters in the oceans are billfish, including the blue marlin and sailfish. They can swim at 81 miles per hour (130 kph), which is as fast as a high-powered speedboat.
• A single humpback whale (left) can eat up to 2.2 tons (2,000 kg) of herring in a day: the weight of two small cars.
• When shoals of tuna attack their prey, the scent of blood in the water can attract hungry sharks from more than 3,280 feet (1,000 m) away.

A humpback whale bursts up through the ocean surface, scooping up a huge mouthful of fish.

BAIT BALLS

The shoals of small fish attract bigger fish such as tuna and sharks, as well as dolphins and fish-eating whales. These attack the shoals, which try to defend themselves by forming tight, swirling "bait balls" of fast-swimming fish. As the ocean hunters attack from below, seabirds such as gannets and albatrosses swoop down from the sky to snatch them from just below the surface. The amazing flying fish may even try to escape by air, only to be picked off by low-flying, long-billed frigate birds.

LOCATION FILE

THE SOUTHERN OCEAN

One of the most food-rich oceans is also one of the coldest: the Southern Ocean that surrounds Antarctica. It contains millions of tons of shrimp-like krill, which swim in such vast swarms that they can color the ocean red. The krill are eaten by huge numbers of fish, seals, penguins, and whales.

Above: A "bait ball" of small shoaling fish makes an irresistible feast for a hungry blue shark.

THE DARK DEPTHS

Food is hard to find in the deep ocean, below the sunlit surface waters. So although this region makes up most of the living space in an ocean, only a small proportion of the ocean wildlife actually lives there. These animals are some of the strangest on the planet.

THE TWILIGHT ZONE

Most ocean life lives in the top 656 feet (200 m) of water, where sunlight allows the clouds of plankton to provide food for fish and other animals. Below this level lies the **twilight zone**, where the only light is a faint blue glow. But animals do live here, and many retreat to this shadowy region during the day to hide from their enemies. They include tiny shrimp-like animals, fish, and even whales.

Many animals that live in the twilight zone have big eyes so they can see in the gloom. They are often silvery or transparent, and some produce a faint blue light called **bioluminescence** that matches the glow from above, so they are harder to see. But some hunters are able to tell the difference between the two types of light, and others even have bioluminescent "headlights" of their own for lighting up their prey.

FACT FILE

DEEP OCEAN GIANTS

Most of the animals that live in the dark depths are very small, but some are giants. They include the giant squid (left), which can be at least 49 feet (15 m) long. Its huge eyes are the size of dinner plates. The squid is hunted by the mighty sperm whale, which grows to 59 feet (18 m). It can dive to 3,280 feet (1,000 m) or more on one breath of air.

This giant squid (*Architeuthis dux*) was found washed up on a beach in Tasmania.

BLACK SMOKERS

Some of the most amazing places in the deep ocean are the "black smokers" on mid-ocean ridges. They are underwater geysers, which gush black, mineral-rich water that has been heated to 662 °F (350 °C) or more. They support forms of life that are found nowhere else on Earth, including giant marine worms up to seven feet (2 m) long.

The mineral-rich water that pours from a black smoker is heated to incredibly high temperatures by contact with hot volcanic rock.

THE DARK DEPTHS

Below 3,280 feet (1,000 m), there is no light at all. Most of the animals that live here eat dead plankton and other things that drift down from above, but some are hunters. They find their prey by sensing movement in the water. They may have to wait for days for a meal, so they have huge mouths, long teeth, and elastic stomachs, enabling them to eat anything they find.

The deep ocean floor may be 9,840 feet (3,000 m) or more below the twilight zone. Starfish, crabs, marine worms, and even some fish live here, eating any dead food that drifts to the bottom. It is a cold, dark, mysterious world, which humans still know little about.

Like many fish that hunt in the depths, the viperfish has long, needle teeth to make sure it catches its prey.

35

OCEAN TOURISM

The depths of the oceans have been visited by only a few scientists. But the ocean surface is like a magnet for tourists. Every year thousands of people go on ocean cruises, set off on sea voyages in yachts, enjoy whale-watching trips, or go reef-diving for close encounters with ocean wildlife.

EXPLORATION AND ESCAPE

The oceans are wild and dangerous, but they are also incredibly beautiful. For many people, a week or two spent exploring part of the ocean makes a perfect escape from their ordinary lives. Some take vacations on big cruise ships, others learn how to sail and navigate small yachts over long distances. A few have sailed around the world, following the routes pioneered by early explorers such as Magellan and Drake.

Tourists on a whale-watching trip have a close encounter with an orca, or killer whale.

LOCATION FILE

WHALE WATCHING

Kaikora, in South Island, New Zealand, lies on the edge of the South Pacific Ocean. The water is rich in minerals and plankton, and attracts huge whales such as humpbacks, sperm whales, and orcas. Boat trips from the shore allow visitors to get close to the whales for an amazing view of these giants.

The steel mesh of a shark cage can seem very flimsy when a person is faced with a great white shark.

DIVING TO ADVENTURE

Many people are more interested in the ocean wildlife. Some go on long boat trips to watch whales, dolphins, and giant basking sharks. A few even go on working vacations, to help scientists with their research into ocean animals and help conserve ocean environments.

One of the biggest advances in ocean research was the invention of SCUBA gear, which stands for Self-Contained Underwater Breathing Apparatus. At first, this was used mainly by scientists, but today there are sport diving clubs all over the world. Every year thousands of divers head for tropical oceans to dive over the coral reefs and enjoy the beautiful corals and reef fish. Special diving suits even allow divers to explore beneath the polar pack ice.

IN THE SHARK CAGE

In some oceans, divers risk being attacked by sharks. But even this is exciting for some people, who go on special shark-diving trips. In places where the sharks are particularly dangerous, divers are lowered into the water in shark-proof steel cages. They may even have a close encounter with a great white shark, which is probably the most deadly creature in the ocean.

PEOPLE FILE

ELLEN MACARTHUR

Ellen Macarthur was just 18 when she sailed around Britain single-handed. She went on to sail across the Atlantic in 33 days, in a yacht just 21 feet (6.4 m) long. Then she raced around the world non-stop in a 49-foot (15 m) yacht called Kingfisher. In the course of her voyages, Macarthur has been at sea in some of the worst storms in the world.

MINERAL RICHES

All kinds of valuable minerals lie on or under the ocean floor. Some have already been gathered, but others are too difficult to get at. They would cost more to collect than they are worth. But one day, people may find easier, cheaper ways of mining the oceans.

OIL AND NATURAL GAS

One of the world's most valuable products is oil. It is used as fuel to make electricity, and it is turned into gasoline. It is also made into plastics. The natural gas that collects above oil reserves is used as fuel for heating and cooking.

Oil and natural gas form in rocks below ground and can be reached by drilling oil wells. But a lot of the world's oil and gas reserves lie under the seabed. To get at them, engineers build drilling platforms that stand in up to 1,312 feet (400 m) of water. These platforms are hugely expensive, but the oil and gas are so valuable that they are worth the expense.

LOCATION FILE

THE NORTH SEA OILFIELDS

There are about 150 oil and gas drilling platforms in the North Sea, between Britain and mainland Europe. Each year, the oil platforms produce about 165 million tons (150 million t) of oil. The oil and gas are pumped through long pipes from rock between 2,952 and 16,400 feet (900–5,000 m) below the seabed.

Flares of waste gas burn brightly against the sky at this oilfield in the Gulf of Mexico.

Ocean winds can be used to power turbines that generate electricity, like these in the sea off Denmark.

FACT FILE

OIL AND GAS

- Almost two-thirds of the world's energy, including electricity, comes from oil and natural gas.
- Every year, the world uses at least 1,760 million tons (1,600 million t) of oil.
- About a third of the oil and gas is drilled from beneath the sea, using oil platforms standing on the continental shelves.

DEEP-OCEAN WEALTH

Oil and gas are drilled from beneath the shallow water of the continental shelves. But the deep oceans also hold mineral riches. Large areas of the ocean floor are covered with fist-sized lumps of valuable metals such as manganese, cobalt, nickel, and copper. They are worth a fortune, but since they lie at least 13,120 feet (4,000 m) below the surface, they are not worth the trouble of gathering up. Even the ocean water itself is valuable. It contains precious metals, including gold! But colossal amounts of water have to be processed to get a tiny weight of gold, so it's not done.

SEA POWER

The oceans could be more valuable as a source of electricity. Waves, tides, and ocean winds can be used to drive electricity generators. And as oil and gas become more difficult to find, people may need these alternative sources of energy.

OCEAN FISHERIES

For centuries, humans have gathered fish from the oceans. Fishing is a form of hunting, because the fish are wild. Provided the fish can breed fast enough to replace the ones that are caught, fishing can go on forever. But if too many fish are caught, the fish stocks eventually disappear.

FISHING TECHNIQUES

People catch ocean fish using all kinds of techniques. Some fish are caught on hooks and lines. One method, called longlining, involves trailing up to 20,000 hooks on a line up to 74 miles (120 km) long!

Other fishing boats use nets. Trawl nets are like huge socks that are hauled through the water to scoop up fish. Drift nets hang from floats at the surface like curtains, catching fish that swim in shoals. Another type of net, called a purse seine, is set in a circle around a fish shoal. When the fish are inside, the bottom is drawn together to make a bag, so the shoal can be lifted out of the water.

Oceanic fish like these tuna were once out of reach of the fishing fleets, but modern ocean-going fishing boats have changed that.

LOCATION FILE

SOUTHERN OCEAN SLAUGHTER

A big problem with modern fishing is that other animals, such as dolphins, seals, and turtles, get caught in the nets and drown. In the Southern Ocean, boats catching fish on baited longlines also catch albatrosses and other seabirds. The birds try to snatch the bait but get hooked and dragged underwater. Up to 100,000 seabirds are killed like this every year in the Southern Ocean alone, including 10,000 to 20,000 albatrosses.

HIGH TECHNOLOGY

Modern fishing boats know exactly where to find fish, thanks to electronic echo-sounders that use sound signals (sonar) to detect fish below the boat. Big boats are also able to process the fish and freeze it, so they don't need to return to shore with their fresh catch. They can stay at sea for months, and travel long distances to reach remote oceans. They return with their fish cleaned, frozen, or even canned.

OVERFISHING

All of this technology has made fish easier to catch than ever. But if whole shoals of fish are scooped from the oceans, they cannot breed and produce more fish. This sort of overfishing has made many types of fish rare, and could destroy them altogether. So fishing is now strictly controlled to prevent this from happening, but the controls have forced many boats to give up fishing.

Commercial whaling almost wiped out many species of whales before it was stopped, largely thanks to conservation groups such as Greenpeace.

 FACT FILE

FISHING FACTS

• Every year, more than 83 million tons (75 million t) of fish and shellfish are caught in the world's oceans.

• About one-third of this is frozen, or sold fresh for human food.

• Another third is canned, or preserved by being dried or smoked.

• The rest is used to make fish oil, or ground up to make animal feed or even **fertilizer** for farm crops.

POLLUTING THE OCEANS

Over the years, the oceans have become more and more polluted with garbage. Some is trash that gets thrown away or swept off ships, such as plastic bottles and bits of fishing net. But the water is also polluted with chemicals and sewage. Both types of pollution can be deadly to ocean life.

A LOAD OF GARBAGE

The oceans are full of all sorts of garbage. Some is there by accident, like the oil that spills from wrecked ships. But a lot is dumped on purpose. Some factories built near the coast get rid of their chemical waste by pumping it out to sea through long pipelines. Others dump it in rivers that flow into the sea. Sewage is often pumped into the sea without being treated first. And sometimes drums of dangerous chemicals are taken out and dumped in the deep ocean. There are three main kinds of ocean pollution: solid trash, poisonous chemicals, and waste organic matter such as sewage and farm fertilizers.

ENDANGERING WILDLIFE

Most of the solid trash is made of various sorts of plastic, which does not break down like paper or wood. A nylon net lost from a fishing boat can float in the ocean for 50 years or more, and during that time it keeps catching and killing fish. This sort of trash can also entangle and drown seabirds, seals, dolphins, and turtles.

Dangerous chemicals include oil, pesticides that have been washed off farmland into rivers, waste chemicals from factories, and even radioactive waste from nuclear power plants. All of these things can poison ocean wildlife.

A discarded fishing net is a death trap for animals like this seal, which will drown or starve if it is not rescued.

OIL SPILLS
• About 3.8 million tons (3.5 million t) of oil spill into the oceans every year.
• Roughly one-tenth of this oil comes from shipwrecked tankers. In 2002, for example, the damaged oil tanker Prestige spilled about 5,500 tons (5,000 t) of oil onto the Spanish coast.
• The rest of the spilled oil—about 3.3 million tons (3 million t)—comes from oilfield accidents and deliberate dumping.

Oil spilling from this wrecked tanker in 2001 threatened the unique wildlife of the Galápagos Islands, a world-famous nature reserve in the Pacific.

DEADLY SEWAGE
The most common form of pollution is raw sewage from coastal towns. When it gets into the ocean, it acts like fertilizer on the phytoplankton, making it grow extra-fast. But this type of "plankton bloom" can be deadly, because it often produces poisons that can kill millions of fish.

Sewage pouring into the sea from this pipe could trigger a deadly plankton bloom.

LOCATION FILE

THE MEDITERRANEAN
Every year, about 440 million tons (400 million t) of raw sewage are pumped into the Mediterranean Sea. This can make the water dangerous to swim in, and it can also cause poisonous plankton blooms. The problem is made worse because water cannot flow in and out of the Mediterranean easily, so most of the sewage stays where it is dumped.

OCEAN FUTURES

Sea levels and ocean currents have stayed roughly the same for 8,000 years, since the world warmed up after the last ice age ended. But modern air pollution is warming up the planet even more, and the effects of this on the world's oceans could change everyone's life.

THE GREENHOUSE EFFECT

Every year, huge amounts of carbon dioxide gas are pumped into the atmosphere around Earth. The gas is produced by burning fossil fuels, such as coal, oil, natural gas, and gasoline. People burn the fuel in car engines, in central heating, and in power plants that make the electricity people use in their homes.

The carbon dioxide in the atmosphere works much like the glass of a greenhouse. It lets the heat of the sun through, but stops it from escaping again. This is called the greenhouse effect. Since the heat cannot get out, a greenhouse warms up in the sunshine. The same thing is happening to the planet. This is called global warming.

RISING OCEANS

Global warming could have a dramatic effect on the oceans. When water warms up, it expands, or takes up more room. So sea levels all over the world are rising. They have risen by up to 7.8 inches (20 cm) over the past 100 years, and may rise a lot more, causing serious flooding.

Scientists analyzing Arctic ice have found that the level of carbon dioxide in the atmosphere has risen in line with global warming, and may well be its cause.

The low-lying coral islands of the Maldives would be among the first casualties of rising sea levels caused by global warming.

THE MALDIVES

The Maldives, in the Indian Ocean, is an island nation of 1,300 islands (above). These were created by coral reefs growing on extinct underwater volcanoes. The land is only seven feet (2 m) above sea level at most, so if the level rises with global warming, the Maldives will gradually disappear beneath the waves.

Strange things could also happen to the ocean currents. These affect the weather, so there could be more storms, droughts, and other disasters— or there could be fewer. The warm current that washes around Europe might slow down, so the European climate would get colder. No one actually knows what will happen, and experts differ in their predictions. But scientists do agree that the future of the oceans could be quite dramatic, for everyone.

GLOSSARY

Algae Plant-like living things that live in the oceans, and other wet places. Some are microscopic and float in the water, and others are usually called seaweeds.

Basalt A dark, heavy rock that forms most of the ocean floor.

Bioluminescence A faint blue light produced by some animals that live in the twilight zone of an ocean.

Continental drift The way the continents have moved around the globe over millions of years.

Continental shelf The edge of a continent, flooded with ocean water.

Continents Big sheets of rock that are lighter than the rock that makes up the ocean floor and rise above the oceans as dry land.

Crust The brittle, rocky shell of Earth.

Currents Flows of ocean water.

Echo-sounders Machines that measure water depth (or locate fish) using sound signals and their echoes.

El Niño A seasonal change in the ocean currents in the eastern Pacific at the equator, which warms up the water and stops the plankton from growing.

Fertilizer A substance spread on farmland to help plants grow.

Gulf Stream A warm current that flows northeast across the Atlantic, from Florida to western Europe.

Ice age A very cold period in Earth's history.

Magnetometers Devices that measure magnetism.

Mantle The thick layer of hot rock below Earth's crust.

Mid-ocean ridge A place where hot rock from the mantle erupts to form oceanic crust, creating a double chain of submarine mountains.

Minerals Chemical substances, usually forming crystals, found in rocks; some minerals form rocks. Plants absorb minerals from soil or water and use them to make living tissue.

Ocean floor The bottom of the deep ocean, made of basalt covered with ooze.

Ocean trenches Deep chasms in the ocean floor, caused by one plate of Earth's crust sliding beneath another.

Orbiting Circling Earth. The moon orbits Earth.

Phytoplankton Plankton consisting of algae.

Plankton Living things, often microscopic, that float in the ocean water.

Pollution Anything that spills into the air or water, and is not part of its natural chemistry, such as poisonous chemicals and sewage.

Rift valley A valley created when Earth's crust rips apart.

Satellites Objects, often man-made, that circle Earth in orbit.

Sewage Human waste and drainage water.

Submersible A small submarine designed for scientific research, and often able to explore very deep water.

Tides Twice-daily movements of ocean water, caused by the gravity of the moon.

Tropics The hottest parts of the world.

Twilight zone The part of the deep ocean that is lit by faint blue light, above the dark zone, where there is no light at all.

Upwelling zones Parts of the ocean where water rich in minerals is drawn up from the ocean floor.

Zooplankton Animals, often very small, that float in the ocean water.

FURTHER INFORMATION

WEB SITES TO VISIT

http://www.divediscover.whoi.edu

An interactive tour of mid-ocean ridges and
underwater volcanoes, with pictures and videos shot
from deep-water submersibles.
Woods Hole Oceanographic Institution
Information Office
Co-op Building, MS #16
Woods Hole, MA 02543
Tel: (508) 548-1400
E-mail: information@whoi.edu

http://www.oceanexplorer.noaa.gov

The Web site of the U.S. National Oceanic and
Atmospheric Administration, all about ocean
exploration technology and wildlife.
NOAA Public Affairs
U.S. Department of Commerce
14th Street and Constitution Avenue, NW
Room 6217
Washington, D.C. 20230
Tel: (202) 482-6090
E-mail: oceanexplorer@noaa.gov

http://www.mcsuk.org

The Web site of the UK Marine Conservation
Society, with information on current problems
and campaigns.
UK Marine Conservation Society
9 Gloucester Road
Ross-on-Wye
Herefordshire HR9 5BU, UK
Tel: 01989 566017
E-mail: info@mcsuk.org

BOOKS TO READ

Farndon, John. *How the Earth Works*. Pleasantville, N.Y.:
Reader's Digest Association, 1992.

Fothergill, Alistair, et al. *The Blue Planet.* New York: DK
Publishing, 2002.

Kunzig, Robert. *Mapping the Deep: The Extraordinary
Story of Ocean* Science. New York: W. W. Norton and
Company, 2000.

MacQuitty, Miranda. *Ocean*. New York: DK Publishing,
2000.

INDEX